Dedication

To my daughter Evelyn,

May you find your inner light in the darkness,
shine brightly in the shadows,
and spread your rays in the storms—
Be you and stay true.

With love and light,
Mama

All Rights Reserved. Copyright 2019. Bee Free
Text by Jolene Burch & Illustrations by Agne Alaburdaite

Mindful Adventures

BEE FREE

Written by
Jolene Burch

Illustrated by
Agne Alaburdaite

"Hi! I'm Suzee Bumble Bee
and that's my Mama Busy Bee.

She says she has no time to play,
but all I want to do today,

Is spend some time just flying free—
We'll laugh together, happily."

-Suzee

Bumble Bee Breath

Let's pretend to be bumble bees! Sit down, take a deep breath in, and say "buzzzzz" while bending forward to reach for your toes. Continue to breathe and buzz until you feel calm and ready to begin our adventure together.

"Let's leave behind the busy nest,
enjoy this sunny day, and rest!

The clouds are fluffy mounds of fun
that float beneath the shining sun.

We'll ride up to the giant moon
by flying on a big balloon!"

-Suzee

Hot Air Balloon Ride

Let's blow up a hot air balloon together. Take a big breath in then exhale slo-o-o-o-wly to blow up the balloon you're holding in your hands. The more you blow, the bigger the balloon will be and the higher it will go. Soon, we will be floating away!

"If sudden storms come rolling in,
we'll use our strength that lies within,

To trust that we can just let go
and ride along the windy blow.

The leaves will sail us to the trees,
to shelter there and rest with ease."

-Mama

Easy Breezy Leaves

While we wait for the storm to pass, let's play a game! Open one hand wide like a leaf and trace each finger one at a time. Breath in on the way up, hold your breath at your fingertip, and breath out on the way down. Continue until you have traced all your fingers. Look, the worst of the storm has passed!

Blooming Buds

Let's grow fragrant flowers for the garden. Make a small "O" with your hand. This will be your flower bud. Now, flick open one finger petal at a time: 1 (pointer)- 2 (middle)- 3 (ring)- 4 (pinky)- 5 (thumb). Repeat on your other hand. When we're done, we will have huge blooming flowers that smell so nice!

Ohm, Fishy-Fishy

Let's go scuba diving and find some ohm fish! Breathe in deeply, then plug your nose and sink down under the water. Call the ohm fish over to you by saying "Ohmmmmm." The longer we call, the closer they will come to us.

Goodnight Light

Let's search for lightning bugs to brighten up our night. Catch a lightning bug with two hands and bring it to your heart. Catch more and more until you feel full of light. Remember to let the lightning bugs go free and thank them for sharing their light with us.

"The sky has faded blue to gray,
to settle down our fun-filled day.

With one last flight, we'll soar up high—
Where stars shine brightly in the sky.

Of all the little bees, it's true,
not one will ever be like you."

-Mama

Rock-a-bye Star

Let's be calm tonight so we can shine like stars so bright! Lie on your back and grab a foot with each hand. Relax and rock your body from side to side while breathing slo-o-o-o-owly in and out. The more we breathe, the calmer we will be, and the longer we rock, the brighter we will become!

About the Author

Jolene Burch is a wife, mother, pediatric occupational therapist, holistic health consultant, and mindset mentor. After experiencing an early career burnout, she sought a transformational journey to find more balance and connect with her daughter in order to heal on a deeper level. She believes that obstacles offer individuals the opportunity to change what does not work for them, and follows the principles of positive and conscious parenting. Jolene is passionate about helping other families grow together by sharing her techniques and writings.

www.ingramcontent.com/pod-product-compliance
Lightning Source LLC
Chambersburg PA
CBHW040301100526

44584CB00004BA/314